Break the Press

Positioning Yourself for Success

Break the Press

Positioning Yourself for Success

by L.T. Willis

Editor
Ray Glandon

Proofreader
Televijay Technologies

Senior Editor
Tracy Duprey

Senior Publisher
Steven Lawrence Hill Sr.

ASA Publishing Company
ASA Publishing Corporation

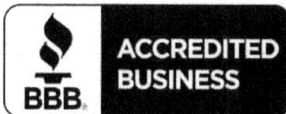

A Publisher Trademark Cover page

ASA Publishing Company
An Accredited Publishing House with the BBB

105 E. Front St., Suite 101
Monroe, Michigan 48161
www.asapublishingcompany.com

Copyrights©2014 L.T. Willis, All Rights Reserved
Book: Break the Press"
Date Published: 06.14
Edition: 1 / *Trade Paperback*
Book ASAPCID: 2380649
ISBN: 978-1-886528-82-6
Library of Congress Cataloging-in-Publication Data

This book was published in the United States of America.
State of Michigan

A Publisher Trademark Title page

Table of Contents

ACKNOWLEDGMENTS

I would like to thank my beautiful wife, Kimberly, for allowing me the time to listen and to write for God. You are truly the significant piece to the puzzle of life that makes me complete. I would like to thank my children for their patience and their understanding of the meaning, "The door to Daddy's office is closed."Many thanks to my parents, Rev. Arthur C. Willis, Sr., (Senior Pastor of the Pentecost Missionary Baptist Church in Romulus, MI) and Lady Janice Willis for showing me the way of the Lord at a very young age. I thank my siblings who have each been an inspiration to me with their unending support. In addition, I'd also like to acknowledge a long list of pastors, ministers, family and friends who have continued to encourage me in all my writings. I thank Ray Glandon for his continuing guidance as a writer and a friend. I would also like to thank Steven Hill and ASA Publishing. Lastly, to all the teachers that I've ever had in christian education, grade school, and college, the lessons you've taught have been priceless in shaping me as a teacher, writer, and mentor.

I dedicate this book to those who are and who have been trapped by the enemy. I pray that by reading this book, you will take a stand to "break the press" and position yourself for success.

From the Editor:

I've had an editor/author relationship with L.T. for a number of years. It's been my pleasure to observe an honorable, life-loving person who generally cares about the world around him and wishes to share his experiences and knowledge. His insight and analysis show keen awareness of the enemy waiting to prey and press and the remedies necessary to combat and break the press. Read for yourselves.

Ray Glandon, Editor.

Break the Press

Positioning Yourself for Success

by L.T. Willis

Introduction

It was the year 1999. I was a sophomore on the junior varsity (JV) basketball team at Ferndale High School. We were into our season of conference play, and, as usual, there were certain schools that we had circled on the calendar in our locker rooms and on our refrigerators at home. A couple of these schools were rivals, and some we just didn't like. For the most part, these schools didn't like us either, so the feelings were mutual. On this particular night, the school we were going to play did not like us at all.

It was a Friday night, and we were on the road against Southfield Lathrup High School. The gym was very hostile! Usually the gym doesn't fill up until the varsity game starts, which is played 20 minutes after the JV game ends. However, this night was different, and in a sea of red and black, the Chargers of Lathrup made sure we knew they didn't like us. Although we weren't on friendly terms with Lathrup, we had a certain high regard for their school because they had a good varsity team as well. We knew our varsity team would do well against them. We respected their program on all levels of competition. However, we couldn't envision the disrespect and dislike that was coming our way.

The score went back and forth for a while. We were playing hard and tough, but we were on the road, so Lathrup played with a lot of momentum. As the game neared the 4th quarter, our coach decided to increase the lead we had because being on the road, in a hostile environment, anything could happen, so a big lead could be the deciding factor in who would win the game.

As the 4th quarter started, "it" happened, the "1" press. One thing that Ferndale basketball was known for was scoring and pressing. If executed properly, our "1" press could literally suck the life out of our opponents. Because we implemented this defense, we had to implement an offense during practices to combat it. In other words, being a good pressing team against ourselves made us good at breaking presses from other teams. A **press** in basketball is a tactic of harassing and incorporating a close guarding defense in which the team without the ball pressures the opponent man-to-man the entire length of the court in order to disrupt dribbling or passing, thereby causing a turnover. This press would literally look like the shape of a diamond. One person would guard the person in-bounding the ball, two people would be on opposite sides of the court at the free-throw line extensions, one person at half-court, and the fifth person at the other end (three point line). Most coaches refer to this press as the Diamond Press (1-2-1-1). We called it "1," and we implemented it after every made basket.

We went on to win that game in decisive fashion, as we pulled away in the 4th quarter. We forced Lathrup to make multiple turnovers. When you're on the road, forcing turnovers is a huge confidence booster, and it causes momentum to shift to the visiting team. Lathrup became very frustrated, and a few players allowed their emotions to get the best of them after the game was over. As we were in line to shake hands, one of their players blind-sided my teammate with a punch to the face. The next thing I knew there was a brawl in the middle of the gym between the two teams. We pressured them so much and their frustration became so overbearing that they lost control of their good character. I will never forget that day. For the remainder of my athletic career in high school, any competition between these two schools was more than a rivalry, it was hatred for some.

This scenario happened years ago, but I've seen similar parallels in life. I've observed some people feeling the pressures of the enemy to be so overwhelming, that they've completely lost it! They've lost all hope, ambition, motivation, and drive for success. From the kindergarten talent show to senior prom, from high school graduation to the present, something went terribly wrong. You felt in your heart that you were going to be this or that, but something tip-toed into your life and forced you to turn that dream over to the enemy. Is Satan pressing you in your life? Does it seem like you just can't get ahead? Have you found yourself out of position? Do you find yourself turning the ball over to the enemy time after time after time? It is my prayer that this book will provide spiritual insight on how to break the enemy's press. Where the Spirit of the Lord is, there is liberty, and Christ has come to set us free from sin, free from bondage, and free from doubt. Don't allow the enemy to press you to a point in your life where you lose it! Some have lost jobs, marriages, homes, children, and other meaningful relationships because of their failure to break the press. Some have started out with great intentions, focusing on living their dreams, but they're stuck because of the very presence of a pressing situation.

As I stated before, although my team was known for implementing a press, we also knew how to break a press very well. There are certain keys to breaking a press that are vital in basketball. First, people who know how to handle the pressure should be on the floor. Handling the pressure means that you're confident in your ability to pass or dribble to certain areas of the floor. You know your next move before you make it. I cannot tell how many times our opponents never got a grip on the ball because they felt the pressure before it was really applied. Secondly, those who are in the best shape should be on the floor. They have trained for that very moment. They're well-conditioned and able to outlast the opponent's endurance. Lastly, those who have a high basketball IQ should be on the floor, people who not only understand the philosophy of the press, but also the press breaker. We had people who knew where the ball had to get and who should or shouldn't be handling the ball.

These same principles and strategies can be applied in our lives. We need a degree of faith that promotes confidence that we will get out of that situation. You can be telling yourself, "I can get through this!" However, the press on your life will be much more difficult if you have little or no conditioning. So many times believers have found themselves to be out-of-shape and easy victim to the enemy. It's no secret that some of the best conditioning comes from running. My friends often say that I'm so busy with church, that I'm running all the time. I'm simply working on my conditioning. I've found that the more I'm involved in ministry, the better my spiritual condition becomes. Furthermore, I have on countless occasions heard legendary athletes of the National Basketball Association (NBA) attribute their success to being "in-shape" and being a student of the game.

To go along with spiritual conditioning, biblical IQ, as it relates to knowledge and application, will certainly benefit us in breaking the enemy's press on our lives. What this means is that you should want to frequent bible studying and christian education opportunities as much as possible. What's absolutely important to keep in mind while reading this book, *Break the Press,* is that as soon as you begin to live on purpose, the enemy will try and force you to commit turnovers, giving the ball to the other team. The ball is your purpose, and your destination is the goal. While this book is not an attempt to tell you that you'll automatically be successful when you break the enemy's press on your life, it does suggest that you'll be positioning yourself to be successful. There are other components that need to play out for you to score, which only God controls. However, with this book, you'll have the training and IQ to be in position! You'll not only recognize a press when it's coming, but you'll also understand that a press is simply a scheme of traps. When you figure out how not to get trapped, you'll know how to break the press and position yourself for success.

PART 1

CHAPTER 1

It's More than a Game, It's a War:

For the weapons of our warfare are not of the flesh, but have divine power to destroy strongholds.
II Corinthians 10:4 ESV

Games promote fun. At the end of the day, no hard feelings should be kept. However, I can tell you that some basketball games that I have played have felt like battles, leaving many with bad feelings. Just ask the Chicago Bulls and the Detroit Pistons during the NBA playoffs in the late 1980s. I'm sure Michael Jordan or Isaiah Thomas would testify that these games were more than recreation. It was a war! Unfortunately, some of us have taken the "game" approach with our spirituality as it relates to our faith in Christ. Believe me when I tell you that Satan is perfectly fine with you approaching your faith as recreation. He keeps pressing, and you're completely comfortable with losing battle after battle because you have the "it's just a game" mentality. But, when you're ready to break out of the traps that have been set before you, you'll develop the, "this means war" mentality.

Whether it's a game or a war, both players and soldiers must identify those involved in battle and recognize who is friend or foe. Whose team are you on? Whom are you battling with ... God or Satan? Let's identify the key players: You, God, and the Enemy.

Finding out who you are can be trivial depending on where you've found yourself to be in life. Some of us know from the day we've matured in faith who we are, and we have embraced that identity. Others don't find out until they've been through a storm or two in life. Moreover, there are some who have yet to discover their identity. We'll deal more with this later in the coming chapters.

The second person we need to identify is God. Who is God? Without overcomplicating it, He is simply the sole maker and ruler of heaven and earth. He is an infinite, Holy and intelligible Spirit. His being is constituted of the Holy Trinity: God the Father, God the Son (Jesus), and God the Holy Spirit. Just as solids, liquids, and gases are defined as matter, God, Jesus, and the Holy Spirit are supernaturally defined as Lord.

The third person we need to identify is the Enemy. He is the great adversary of God and humankind. He is also known as Satan (the Devil). Satan is the opponent, and his defense is well known. He wants to steal, destroy, and kill anything that belongs to God. He wants to steal our lives, destroy our hope, and kill our dreams. He accomplishes this by distracting us into thinking that our spiritual life is a game. This is not a game! This is a war!

Strongholds ...

When it comes down to X's and O's, it's very abstract; you have to label things as they are, teammate or opponent. If you're on God's team, then be reminded that He has trained you through tests and trials to have the ability to break away from any stronghold. Let's take a minute here to define and identify these strongholds. The word speaks for itself, but I'd like to refer to strongholds as vices.

As a child, I had several bikes. My dad would always come home with bikes that he found, and then he'd fix them. I always had company on the weekends, and in those days riding bikes was the thing to do. These bikes weren't brand new, so my dad would do some repairs on them to make them functional. I wasn't (and I'm still not) an expert in tool handling, but my dad would be on the ground working on inner tubes, wheels, pedals, and chains, and he would sometimes call for me to bring him the vise grips. At that age, I didn't really know the purpose of vise grips; All I knew is that he'd use them when he couldn't get a bolt loose. As I got older, I learned there were wrenches and pliers designed to fit nuts and bolts. However, rusts, wear, and tear made it extremely difficult to loosen bolts. The vise grip's function was to lock the bolt in place, making it easier to loosen. Once the lock pressure was applied, the only thing that could get the vise grips to loosen was the release lever. I have found many of us trying to cope with a vice grip in our lives, wishing we could find the release lever. Whether it's men, women, sex, drugs, alcohol, money, gambling, or immorality, the vice grips have taken hold of our lives and locked on, trapping us. We must label those things which are detrimental to our purpose in life as vices (strongholds).

Many have tried to walk in victory while holding hands with a vice, effectively disabling their purpose. When two people are observed holding hands, it generally symbolizes a functional relationship filled with moments of joy. When my wife and I are out for a walk, our holding hands most likely tell observers that we happily belong to each other. When there are moments of unhappiness, we may not be observed holding hands. When you're holding hands with a vice, you're communicating to the world that you belong to that vice. This is right where the Enemy wants you, but there is still hope.

No one is without vices, but that fact doesn't have to paralyze and disqualify you from life. In fact, having a vice means you're very much qualified for the omnipresent sovereignty of God. Just in case you forgot, every vise grip is designed with a release lever directly inside of the handle. If scripture holds true that in every temptation there's a way of escape, then it makes perfectly good sense that God is just as much our release lever as the vise's. 1 Corinthians 10:13 (NLT) says:

"The temptations in your life are no different from what others experience. And God is faithful. He will not allow the temptation to be more than you can stand. When you are tempted, He will show you a way out so that you can endure."

The Enemy will pressure you to a point where you feel weak and trapped, ultimately losing hope. This is right where he wants you. Life is not a game, contrary to how it may be perceived. It is only on the video game that you can start over where you left off if you've saved your information. The key word here is "saved." That's something that you must ask yourself, are you saved? Salvation is the only thing that will allow you to pick up your life from where you left off. If you haven't saved your information, the words "Game Over" literally means you have to start all over again from scratch. Starting from scratch is for some, staying at scratch, and this is precisely part of the Enemy's strategy, to get you trapped at go. Those with a mere game mentality are okay with this cycle of disappointment. However, those of us who've developed a warfare mentality have at some point become uncomfortable, unconvinced, and unhappy with the entrapments of the Enemy and declare that this is indeed more than a game. It's a war! We must break the press!

CHAPTER 2

It's Your Ball

On this walk of faith, finding out who you really are can be difficult if you've spent most of your time in environments filled with distractions. Take a few moments of spare time and ask yourself this question with a notepad and pen to jot down some answers: Who are you? As you think about this question, I suggest that you shouldn't be solely defined by what you're good at. You may be quite skilled at composing lies (liar), but you shouldn't want to be identified as a liar. You may have to dig deep and answer other questions to come up with a final discovery of who you are. Hopefully, all roads will lead to the fact that you are a child of God. 2 Corinthians 5:17 says:

> "This means that anyone who belongs to Christ has
> become a new person.
> The old life is gone; a new life has begun!" (NLT)

As refreshing as that scripture sounds, it doesn't mean that you now reside in a bubble and the enemy can't touch you. Eventually the pressure of some variable infiltrates the film of that bubble, bursting it! Still, the fact remains that you are in Christ and on God's team, fighting for Him. You have possession of the ball (your purpose), and you're on offense. Scoring won't come easy. The Enemy has it out for you because you've been given a fresh start in Christ. As long as you were on the sidelines, in the locker room, or even in the stands, the enemy didn't bother you much. You had no plans to disrupt his agenda until you decided to give God your life. Satan knows what kind of power God has, and with you now on God's team, he's going to pressure you. Quite frankly, it's his job to do that. While I'm not celebrating the enemy's purpose in this world, I'm encouraged that I'm on his radar. An old pastor once shared this with me, "You'll never become a target until you are perceived as a threat. " With the ball in your hands, you're threatening to score, and the enemy is going to apply pressure. When you start living with purpose, the defense attacks, but stand strong, and remember, you're the threat.

Inbound the ball ...

Don't help the enemy out by hindering yourself. God has placed you in the lineup to score! Before that can happen, you must in-bound the ball. You have to live! The last thing you should do is give the enemy momentum by getting a 5-second violation. In basketball, the player has 5 seconds to put the ball into play (pass the ball from out-of-bounds). Not doing so is a violation, and momentum shifts to your opponent. Life is full of opportunities, and we can't afford to miss the window. God says He'll open up the windows of heaven and pour us out blessings that we won't have room enough to receive (Malachi 3:10). Time is ticking, and some have become so fragile by the very presence of pressure that they've committed turnovers before ever giving themselves a chance to live. Yes, not in-bounding the ball means the other team gets the ball.

Living a life without a handle on your purpose means that the enemy will take over. Have you ever met someone who said they wanted to live for Christ and wanted to be successful in life, but once exposed to potential challenges, they folded and fell into the hands of the enemy? This was me. I thought the stipulations of being a Christian were too much at a young age, that I had time to start living for Christ later in life. I was young, and I wanted to explore my youth. I chose clubs over church, bars over bible studies, drinks over dreams, and women over worship. I knew the key players, but at the time, I had the mentality that this was a game. I didn't realize Satan was destroying me in the points-off-of-turnovers category (scoring because of turnovers). I actually had zero points because I never put the ball into play. I had on the uniform, I looked ready on "game-day," but the pressures of living a life for Christ killed me before I even lived. I didn't realize the clock was ticking and I was the one responsible for the turnovers in my life. What about you? What are you doing with the ball?

I'm reminded of the parable that Jesus told in Matthew 25: 15-30 (NLT). The servant who received one bag of silver and hid it in the ground, doing nothing with it, became a great disappointment to his master. He was thrown into outer darkness and was disqualified from living because he made the reckless decision not to put to use what his master had given him.

"To those who use well what they are given, even more
will be given, and they will have an abundance.
But from those who do nothing, even what little they have
will be taken away.

Now throw this useless servant into outer darkness,
where there will be weeping and gnashing of teeth."
(Matt. 25:29-30 NLT)

The purpose that God has put on your life has great meaning. Don't allow your fear of the pressures from the enemy to deter and disrupt your decision to inbound your purpose, to break the press and position yourself to score. You're the threat, and if the enemy can make you forget that, he wins the battle before it even gets started. The press is breakable. Put your purpose in pursuit. The clock is ticking!

Chapter 3

It's a Trap! Protect the ball.

One of the first things a basketball player learns is the importance of protecting the basketball. If you fail to learn this skill, you'll commit what is called a turnover. You give the enemy possession to that which was yours. Your loss is another's gain, and in this case the enemy is the beneficiary.

We mustn't be careless with our purpose in life. As a child, my dad always reminded me not to tell people everything about myself. Even today I hold that principle close to the heart. It wasn't that he wanted me to be a secretive person, but he knew some things that I hadn't yet experienced in my childhood, things my mind simply wasn't ready to comprehend. Life has taught me that the enemy will turn the pressure of his attack so high, that he disguises his attempts of theft. In other words, you thought you could talk to that family member or friend about things that were private and personal about you, but they betrayed your confidence and used it for their own gain. It helps to have your guard up and to be on the lookout. You can't tell everyone everything. Guard your secrets, and be careful whom you share your strength with. Remember, all traps don't appear to be as they are. Watch for and recognize the schemes.

There's a story in the Bible about the birth of a boy named Samson. Samson was a gift from God to be raised in the fear of the Lord as a Nazirite and to serve as an example to Israel of what their commitment to God should be since they had no leader during this time.

> "You will become pregnant and give birth to a son, and his hair must never be cut. For he will be dedicated to God as a Nazarite from birth. He will begin to rescue Israel from the Philistines."
> Judges 13:5 NLT

Samson grew to be a very mighty man. He killed a young lion with his bare hands. He gathered 300 foxes, tied them together, then sent them through the grain fields with torches in their tails to destroy the crops of the Philistines. He was so strong that on one occasion he broke ropes that bound him. He also killed a thousand Philistines soldiers with a donkey's jawbone. He even carried away the gate of Gaza when the Philistines thought they had trapped him behind the city walls.

Samson's record was almost impeccable, but his life was stained with a vice. He had a weakness for pagan women. Samson found himself trapped once again, but this time he had no ropes to break and no gate to move. He fell into the press of the enemy by simply turning the ball over. We are sometimes to blame for our own entrapment. Samson found himself right where the enemy wanted him.

> Finally, Samson shared his secret with her. "My hair has never been cut," he confessed, "for I was dedicated to God as a Nazarite from birth. If my head were shaved, my strength would leave me, and I would become as weak as anyone else."
> (Judges 16:17 NLT)

Samson's strength was in the length of his hair, and he was never to have it cut. He did well in keeping this a secret until he met Delilah. Samson fell victim to the press of Delilah's quest for the root of his strength, and he found himself cornered! Delilah found his weakness, alerted the Philistines, lured him to sleep in her lap, and had his head shaved. Samson committed a turnover! He turned over his strength right into the hands of the enemy.

This has been a life principle for me, being protective of my strengths. There's a scouting report on your life. The enemy has held countless sessions examining every detail of your life to find a weakness that will cancel out your strength. With our good friend, Samson, the enemy found his weakness to be pagan women, which means a certain relationship was his downfall. Whether it's a friendship or a courtship, relationships can corner us. If not careful, we may allow people into our lives without prior knowledge of their living standards but naively assume that their way of life won't have an effect on us. Satan designs it so that our weakness becomes more attractive and more accessible. We align ourselves with his plan and fall into a trap by connecting with the wrong people. In life, our associations will often determine our ability to avoid being pressured into traps that Satan is planning for our lives. The Enemy knows our weakness and will capitalize on this knowledge to strangle life out of our strength. So, what do you do when your life is under scrutiny and you've come to realize that you're the target? I can hear my college coaches yelling at me even now, "Stay out of the corner!" That's exactly what to do when you know that the enemy has assigned people to try and steal your dreams and make you doubt your purpose. Re-evaluate your relationships and **stay out of the corner**!

In a physical sense, the only time we're in a corner is when we are close to boundaries. The corner of a room is only where both walls meet. The corner in a neighborhood is only when we typically find a perpendicular crossing of streets. In other words, a corner represents a degree of an angle, a 90 degree angle. It is at a 90 degree angle where direction changes. At some point in your life, you may have found yourself to have a change in direction. This is the place of boundary. God has given us righteous boundaries in His word of how we should conduct ourselves as Christians. Paul writes in Romans 12:2 (NLT),

> "Don't copy the behavior and customs of this world, but let God transform you into a new person by changing the way you think. Then you will learn to know God's will for you, which is good and pleasing and perfect."

The boundary has been clearly painted for us much as the baseline and sidelines have been outlined on the basketball court. We have boundaries, but the question is, why are we so close to them? The reality is, we have all at some point flirted with boundaries. Flirtation can be a very dangerous thing. Do you remember that childhood tease when your friends knew you liked a schoolmate? They would run around the playground singing, "Jack and Jill sitting in the tree, k-i-s-s-i-n-g, first comes love, then comes marriage, then comes the baby in the baby carriage!" When I flirted with my wife, we got engaged. After the engagement, came the marriage. After the marriage came the baby in a baby carriage. So we courted one another, got engaged, got married, and then reproduced.

Flirting with boundaries can lead to an engagement, marriage, and reproduction of righteousness. Then we reproduce. Flirting with boundaries can also lead to an engagement, marriage, and reproduction of unrighteousness. This is how some men and women have become married to the streets. They've flirted with boundaries in early adolescence. They've become engaged to the streets by the time they graduate, finding themselves ... on the block (corner). Then they have children who've been reproduced to the block. Many haven't made the decision to go to the corner. In fact, they inherited the corner because the generation before them never made it out. Instead, they settled there.

There's heavy traffic on corners in urban areas of society, and generally that is where deviance can be the greatest. Drug deals, gambling, prostitution, just to name a few, generally market themselves on the corner. As a result, some of our young men and young ladies grow into this trap. Why? Because their outlook on life has been limited to the corner. Frankly, they never see past it, let alone around it. The corner has caused many missed opportunities, and many in our society are being robbed of a good future. There are some great people on the corner. However, the reality remains that it's a corner, and the corner is where people easily become trapped!

In teaching the diamond press-breaker, my coach would explain to us the importance of staying out of the corner. The problem with the corner is that you can't see the entire floor and you may be forced to step out-of-bounds, which is a turnover. The same can be said in life. Ending up in the corner affects your outlook on life, and you will be forced to live life without any boundaries, which is an infraction. When you find yourself cornered, your outlook on life is limited. At one point in time you may have had aspirations of being someone great. You dreamed of being a great wife, great husband, great father, great mother, great doctor, great lawyer, great entertainer, great athlete, great businessman or businesswoman. However, situations have now placed you at a perpendicular point and you've found yourself cornered, not aware of which direction you should be going in life. You've found yourself too close to the boundary, cornered. Now, all of a sudden you're making "now decisions" instead of having "now faith." You've become impulsive in your decision making because it seems like the walls are caving in on you. You're going deeper and deeper into the corner, and you simply can't see your way out. We've seen family members lost to the corner for this very reason. We were on the outside looking in and thought it would be easy for our loved ones to come out of the trap. We didn't realize that, although they could hear us, they simply couldn't see us or a way out. They remained trapped, committing countless turnovers.

Other problems with the corner in the game of basketball are that you're easily guardable and close to the sideline and baseline (boundaries). Flirting with boundaries lead us to being out-of-bounds, and when you're out-of-bounds, you're out of the will of God. When you step out-of-bounds, everything stops and you've lost your purpose to the enemy.

In basketball, when a player steps out of bounds, the clock stops and he loses possession to the other team. Going out-of-bounds is an infraction, and infracted living is a life of irrelevance. Some people have been in the same struggle for years, unable to better themselves. They've stepped out of the will of God into a life without boundaries, spiritually and emotionally conducting themselves any kind of way. When you're in God, it's like being in the game. You are accounted for. Everything you do matters and will ultimately work toward your being successful, as long as you're turnover-free.

In my adolescence, I lived a life playing close to the sideline until one day in my early adulthood I stepped out of bounds. Now you must understand that in most gymnasiums and arenas around the world, the sidelines and baselines on a basketball court are typically decorated with logos and other graphics that beautify and accent the team. However, none of that affects the game, aside from the fact that it is in the out-of-bounds area and where things are irrelevant. In other words, when I stepped out-of-bounds, out of the will of God, it was fun there. I felt free, as if I could do what I wanted when I wanted. In fact, I found that there were a lot more people enjoying themselves off the court, as in basketball, which is where the sidelines and baselines meet the crowd. There's popcorn, candy, food, beer, entertaining cheerleaders and dancers, all out-of-bounds and beyond. When you're living life out-of-bounds, it appears to be unlimited fun and untainted happiness. It's an area of where "everybody's doing it" is the leading mentality. This mentality manifests throughout the game every now and then by the ever famous "wave." I got my first full experience of the "wave" during one of my games in high school where the student section would start throwing both their hands in the air, one section after another, until it made it around the entire gym. I found out in my life that I was simply living on the "wave." I thought I was a leader, but I was just copying what I saw others do before me, just part of a cycle. When the word of God convicted me, I began to examine where I was, not just in life, but in my relationship with Christ. I made the decision to leave the "wave" and learn His will. When we're out-of-bounds, we'll never position ourselves to be successful. When you're cornered, you're too close to the boundaries and flirting with unrighteousness, and that can cause turnovers.

PART 2

CHAPTER 4

The Man in the Middle...

Now that we have been informed of the enemy's scouting report on our lives and all that he plans to do, we must remember some very crucial spiritual tips. It is easy to be consumed with all that is happening in the corner, and we don't know whom to turn to. Quite frankly, you may think a lot of people that you associate yourself with will be around to break you away from the trap, but those people are becoming more difficult to find. Therefore, we're by ourselves looking for a way out, tired of committing turnovers. One thing we learned from our coach was if he couldn't trust you to protect the ball, you were going to find a seat on the bench. God has sent Christ to give us a more abundant life, and the last place a believer should want to be is on the bench. Get in the game, and stay in the game. Can God trust you with your purpose? Or, will you fumble it to the enemy when exposed to pressure?

The enemy is going to press you now that you're representing Christ! Since you have decided to live on purpose, the heat is about to be turned up. But don't worry and become frazzled! There is hope! One of the most important things for us to remember in breaking the press on our lives and positioning ourselves for success is that we're on offense. The Enemy has fooled those in the body of Christ into thinking their lives are supposed to be lived on the defense. This is simply not the case. We're seeking first the Kingdom of God!

"Seek the Kingdom of God above all else, and live righteously, and
He will give you everything you need."
Matthew 6:33 NLT

If the enemy is coming to steal from us, then we must have something that he wants. His desire is to steal our focus on our ambitions by distracting us from seeking God. We possess our purpose, and he wants it. So what do you do when you feel trapped? In basketball the easiest way to avoid a trap is to keep the ball in the middle of the floor. We must place our lives in the hands of Jesus, who is the Man in the middle. I can surely hear that old deacon singing, "He's a burden bearer," or that mother singing, "glory halleluiah since I've laid my burdens down."

Give your burdens to the Lord, and He will take care of you. He will
not permit the godly to slip and fall.
Psalms 55:22 NLT

Jesus is our Lord! He spent His years on earth fulfilling scripture, healing the sick, raising the dead, and giving sight to the blind. Jesus, being the second member of the Holy Trinity, is also our mediator.

For there is only one God and one Mediator who can reconcile God
and humanity—the man Christ Jesus.
1 Timothy 2:5 NLT

As defined in Nelson's New Illustrated Bible Dictionary, a mediator is one who goes between two groups of people to help them work out their differences to come to an agreement.

Jesus alone can bring complete reconciliation because He alone can bring about complete payment for our sin and satisfaction of God's wrath. He sacrificed Himself to secure our redemption and continue to intercede on our behalf. Our prayers are presented to God through His mediation. The Mediator is able to save to the utmost those who come to God through Him. Only you may know the answer as to how you may be in the corner, but allow Christ to mediate on your behalf, and give your life to Him. He's in the middle!

Coach said to keep the ball in the middle of the floor. When you're in the middle, you can see the entire floor, which is your outlook. You can see how the defense is setting up. You are able to recognize the trap before it even comes. Working in Behavior Intervention, one of the things we are taught to do is to conduct a Functional Behavior Analysis on problematic behavior. With this Functional Assessment, we are able to get a better understanding of behaviors and recognize patterns to behaviors, which will always have antecedents, also known as triggers. There is something going on that triggers the behavior. Therefore, we work to be proactive and use preventative strategies to implement a plan to manage the behaviors. The same applies in life. If we would recognize the trap before it comes, perhaps we could be preventative in breaking the press as best as possible so that we're never in position to become trapped in the first place.

In basketball you have to exercise the art of anticipation. Know that it's coming before it comes. Many of us have been in situations where we've been cornered because we failed to anticipate the traps coming. The Enemy has spent an entire practice or two scouting your every move. You owe them the same attention. Recognize the snares of sin before they grab a hold of you and squeeze away your purpose until you're in a dangerous place of irrelevance. The way you anticipate sin is to stay clear of the elements of sin. For example, if you have a gambling problem to the point where it has proved detrimental to your health and wealth, don't go to the casino! If you struggle with alcoholism, don't hang out at the bar! When you remove the element of sin, you're less likely to be enticed and entrapped by the Enemy.

With the ball in the middle of the floor, it's very difficult for the opponent to trap you; however, he will press you. Therefore, there's another benefit to getting the ball to the middle, the Mediator. Having the ball in the middle of the court, you're far from the boundary, and that makes it difficult for the enemy to trap you, and you're less vulnerable to being forced out-of-bounds, the place of irrelevance.

There aren't too many who have been fortunate enough to place their lives in the hands of Christ without being pressured into a trap. As mentioned in earlier chapters, some have inherited the corner. They really had to fight the Enemy since day 1! Generations before them found themselves trapped in the corner and just settled there, finding comfort. Never get comfortable in the corner! God has so much for your life, and you'll never fairly investigate His plan for you from the corner. It's simply too much pressure with too many distractions. If this is you, there is still hope. Because there is a time limit on when we must in-bound the ball and cross half-court in basketball, you don't have time to waste.

While you do have hope, you don't have time to waste. Use the "step-thru."

◆Step-Thru◆

A way to break any trap is to step-through the meeting point of the defenders and advance the ball. The step-thru is located between the two defenders, which is the middle of the trap. The children of Israel used the step-through when they found themselves trapped between Pharaoh's Army and the Red Sea and couldn't get to the wilderness which was the midpoint to Canaan (their destiny).

> Then Moses raised his hand over the sea, and the Lord opened up a path through the water with a strong east wind. The wind blew all that night, turning the seabed into dry land. So the people of Israel walked through the middle of the sea on dry ground, with walls of water on each side!
> Exodus 14:21:22 NLT

God opened the Red Sea to allow the people of Israel to cross over into the wilderness on foot. This is an encouraging message that God can use the elements of our environments to execute our exodus from situations that have us trapped and cornered. Israel simply wouldn't have made it to the wilderness if they hadn't used their feet to step-thru that which was trapping them. When the step-thru is not available, however, you're not out of options. Don't let the devil steal your purpose. There have been many who started out with good intentions and ended up cornered and settled there. This is when the most important strategy should come to mind and lead us to going back to the basics. Get the ball to the middle. In the next chapter, we'll examine what it takes to get the ball back to the middle. However, do not waste time in your consideration because the clock of life is ticking and you don't have time to waste.

◆Back-Court Violation◆

One thing to be mindful of when attempting to break a press in basketball is your awareness of a backcourt violation. **Avoid a Backcourt Violation.** Waiting too long to advance the ball up the court will increase the risk of a turnover. In professional basketball a player has 8 seconds to get the ball across the half court mark. In high school and college basketball the rule is slightly different at 10 seconds. Whether it is 8 seconds or 10 seconds, time is running and you don't have it to waste. Similarly to basketball, people have found themselves wasting time in the backcourt, living their lives backcourt. God has called you out of darkness into His marvelous light. Don't wait too long to make the decision of giving your life to Christ.

One of the biggest mistakes we make in life is thinking that we have time to get our lives in order with God. This is one of the biggest misconceptions of adolescents. They think that because they haven't experienced all the world has to offer that they must take their journey as the Prodigal Son did before they get right with God.

But the day of the Lord will come as unexpectedly as a thief.
Then the heavens will pass away with a terrible noise, and the
very elements themselves will disappear in fire, and the earth and
everything on it will be found to deserve judgment.
2 Peter 3:10 NLT

The fact is, man knows neither the day nor the hour when Christ will return. With that alone, it shaped me years ago to make sure I was working on my relationship with Christ. The fact is, the time is ticking, and we don't have time to waste. So where are you functioning now? How long will you settle in the trap? Wasting time is nothing more than an unforced turnover. You're not allowing yourself to reach your full potential. Therefore, not reaching your full potential in Christ and in life doesn't just affect you, it affects your family as well. Generations will be born into backcourt lifestyles, when from the beginning they were supposed to be front court people. As believers, we know that we are already victorious in Christ, but at the onset of traps and the enemy's pressing, we fail to walk in that victory.

Avoiding a back-court violation will be less of a burden, if at all, once we realize Christ is our guide and the Holy Spirit is our comforter. However, things quickly spiral out of control when we start doing things ourselves. This is equivalent to the basketball player trying to break the full court press all by himself.

Dribble it, Pass it, We Want a Basket

While some players have been tempted to think they can dribble their way out of a press by themselves, it is certainly not advised. The best way to beat a press is to pass the ball. Well, in life, when you try and dribble your way out of the press in your life, you're wasting time. I had a teammate who took great pride in his dribbling skills. We called it "handles." He could do all the tricks with a basketball, but when it was clutch time in basketball games, he wasn't on the floor. In practice, he missed reads to certain plays because of his preoccupation with dribbling the ball and dancing around in the back-court, and he either turned the ball over due to a back-court violation, or he danced his way into a trap. In pressure moments, Coach had very little confidence in him being in the rotation. Although he had nice "handles," he had a habit of dribbling with his head down. When you dribble with your head down, you can't see the entire floor effectively, and you're more vulnerable to dribbling into traps. We have, in some points of our life, dribbled ourselves into traps. You thought you had a handle on your purpose but found yourself dancing right into the trap of the enemy, unaware that the clock never stopped ticking. So now 10 years have passed, and you're still dribbling. When you find yourself being trapped by the enemy, don't dribble it, PASS it!

CHAPTER 5

Reverse the Ball

When we're trapped by the enemy, it appears we're out of options, and there is no seam for a "step-through," it should lead us to re-examine our current situation. One of the most detrimental things a person can do to themselves is to ignore the fullness of their life. What that means is choosing to focus on the surface of their situation rather than examining the entire picture. A few questions I always like to ask myself relative to where I am in life is: how did I get here, where I am going, where do I want to go, and what's stopping me?

How did you get to where you are? This answer will obviously vary from person to person. Some may have simply made bad decisions. Others may have been misled by misperceptions.

Where are you going? To some, the answer to this question is, "nowhere fast." Their future is so clouded by their environment that they can't see brighter days, and as a result, they have no hope for the future and don't know where they want to go.

What's stopping you? It's a good indication that whatever is in that cloud that's blocking you from seeing where you want to go, is the very thing that's stopping you. That cloud could very well be puffed up with people or even yourself.

When it comes to people, you have to literally ask yourself, is this relationship helping me or hurting me, because friends, it is indeed one or the other. There is no in-between.

So where are you in your life? Being accountable for your position in life will allow you to move forward in your thinking. Once you reach this point, you will be able to "reverse the ball."

Reverse does not have to necessarily mean going in the other direction. I'm reminded of how many times I got stuck in the snow when I first learned how to drive. My parents bought me a 1987 Honda Prelude. It was a front wheel drive with a manual transmission. Because my 16th birthday was in February, I had to learn how to drive in the snow. Not only had my dad trained me to drive a manual transmission (stick), he also had to teach me how to maneuver the Honda in the snow. One thing that I learned is that when those front wheels had no traction to go forward, putting the car in reverse while cutting the wheel was my best chance to gain traction to drive forward. Sometimes I had to do this several times in one incident just to make it into a driveway or up a road, nevertheless, it worked! There's really no difference in life. When you do what I've phrased as "reverse the ball," it means you may have to back up, sticking with a plan to go forward.

Reversing the ball back to the middle of the floor is equivalent to getting back into the will of God or giving your life back to Christ! There's a parable that Jesus shares with the Pharisees in Luke 15:11 that shows a young man reversing the ball. This parable in Luke's Gospel is one of a prodigal son or "the lost" son.

> A man had two sons. The younger son told his father, "I want my share of your estate now before you die." So his father agreed to divide his wealth between his sons.
>
> Luke 15:11-12 NLT

He, being called the prodigal, had strayed away from his father's house. The parable represents God as a common father to all mankind, to the whole family of Adam. We are all his offspring, have all one father, and one God who created us. In the 15th verse, this particular son got so far away from home, that he was suppressed by a new master and worked for him in the field. After having been given his portion of wealth and spending it recklessly, he hit rock bottom. He reached such a low point in life that he satisfied his hunger with what the swine ate. Of course, the husks that the swine ate were filling for them, but not for humans; therefore, he turned to begging. And what may have frustrated him most about the situation was when he did beg, no one gave to him. The spiritual significance here is that those who depart from God can't be helped by anything. They have a false sense of help. God gives us eternal help. However, we often try to fill spiritual voids with fleshly desires, which aren't nourishing for the soul. Furthermore, none of them eliminate the problem, but, infact illuminate the problem. Trying to fill spiritual voids with carnal desires brings attention to your issues. The prodigal son reaches this point and realizes that he must reverse the ball.

> When he finally came to his senses, he said to himself, "At home even the hired servants have food enough to spare, and here I am dying of hunger! I will go home to my father and say, "Father, I have

sinned against both heaven and you, and I am no longer worthy to
be called your son. Please take me on as a hired servant."

Luke 15:17-19 NLT

Redemption begins with re-evaluation. The prodigal son was in a transition of reconsideration because while he was sharing meals with pigs, the servants in his father's house were better off than he was. However, what's important to remember is that while there is life, there is hope. Consideration is the first step toward conversion. Every step from backsliding begins with a step back to God. This is the point where the coaching staff would yell, "SWING-IT," implying, reverse the ball. Confession of sin is required as a necessary condition of rebuilding harmony with God. No matter how cornered you are in life, you can always "SWING-IT." Once we get the ball to Christ, then we must fill the lanes as we go forward, positioning ourselves to be successful.

CHAPTER 6

Fast Break

You're now in the best position to score, and chances are you have an advantage because you've broken the press, which means, the ball is ahead of one or more of the defenders. I can't stress how important it is to "fill-the-lane" and run hard. What "fill-the-lane" means is there are three lanes on the basketball court: the middle, and the two wings (one on each side of the middle of the floor). The idea here is that with the ball being in the middle of the floor, and as it moves up the court, the individual with the ball in the middle has an option to pass the ball to his left or his right, depending on which defender (who may have originally been guarding one of the wing players) steps up to guard him. This which would then mean an advantage of a 3 on 2 scenario. When you break a press, you're leaving one or two of the defenders behind and they will be trying to catch up, so that's why it is called a "fast-break." You are to run as hard as you can while remaining in control. We are to do the same in life once we've broken the enemy's press.

You must remember that while you're life is in Christ's hands, it is always ahead of Satan. Christ will always have the upper hand. However, just because it's ahead of Satan, doesn't mean he quit chasing you. He's still trying to catch up with you to impose another trap. Here's where "run as hard as you can" holds spiritual significance. Complacency sometimes settles on the saints of God, to the point where they are lolly-gagging in their pursuit of Christ. This is right where the enemy wants us. Remember, he's seeking whom he may devour. The life of the Apostle Paul is a good study of how we should give the same energy to our purpose in Christ as we did living life out-of-bounds. Some of us ran so hard for the devil, but then we came into the faith of Christ accepting Him as our Savior from sin. We now lack energy and don't run hard for Him. The Apostle worked so diligently at persecuting Christians when he was Saul, but when he was converted to Paul, he kept the same work ethic but changed whom he worked and ran for. He ran hard for Christ and encouraged his mentee, Timothy, to do the same:

> "Work hard so that you can present yourself to
> God and receive His approval.
> Be a good worker, one who does not need to be ashamed
> and who correctly explains the word of truth."
> 2 Timothy 2:15 NLT

Running hard on a fast break gives me the motivation and confidence that I need to be successful. I challenge you to take notice while watching a basketball game and to watch what happens when you see a team on a fast break. Some players' eyes will get bigger. Some will start to "coo" (call) for the ball to be passed to them. Others will wag there tongue. There's something about a fast-break that motivates a team to finish strong, and if done so, momentum will build. Therefore, we can conclude that running hard for Christ will shift momentum our way. And when you have momentum on your side, you'll gain favor. When teams have momentum, calls from the referee will start to work in their favor. The opponent will begin making turnovers, which will cause them to lose their effectiveness. Now we can conclude that when you run hard for Christ, you'll gain momentum on the journey, which will grant you favor, and it's all because you filled-the-lane.

Filling-the-lane means staying in your lane. What that means is once you've opted to fill a specific lane or have been assigned a specific lane, commit to it and be great at it. There's nothing more frustrating than watching someone overstep into your lane and think that they can do your assignment just as well as you if not better, yet failing at it. This has caused several difficulties among many teams in basketball. There's always that one player who think he can dribble the ball well or pass the ball well, but ends up turning the ball over either by losing the ball or throwing an errant pass. Those team's fans groan when they see that player get the ball again out of position. We'd call this person a busy body, all over the place, or in the way. It's important to fill-your-lane and your lane only because it helps you be as successful as possible. Don't mistake being busy to be the same as running hard. Being busy has to do with filling time while running hard has to do with direction, drive, and destiny.

Chapter 7 (Conclusion)

Shoot It, Dunk It!

In the previous chapters, I've outlined an entire possession in the game of basketball including time limits, boundaries, and crowd participation. As long as the game is being played, none of these will go away. The temptation will always remain. The threat of a trap will always be there. You being the target will remain as long as you are perceived as a threat. That fact that you are the target of the Enemy clearly implies that you must be a threat. When you are perceived as threat, there's an alert that will be issued out all over the world to all demons. This is why traps will be set on every side of your life. The pressure will remain. If you've found yourself not being pressed by the Enemy, that could be an indication that you're in no way threatening to score your baskets or achieve your goals.

The game of basketball consists of several possessions. There's a new possession after every made or missed basket and every turnover. You may not get it right the first time. You may not get it right the second time. But, with this recipe for breaking the enemy's press on your spiritual life, you will be in the best position to score the ball. Taking this approach to your spiritual life, you'll position yourself to cash in on your destiny, accomplishing a goal that you've set for yourself. Being from the Midwest, we refer to the basketball rim as the "rim." My family in the South refers to the basketball rim as the "goal." From the time you in-bound the ball, you are trying to make it in the goal. There's no difference in life. You are trying to have your purpose meet up with your destiny at the goal. Whatever goal that might be, there's a winner in you, but winners are only defined by how they finish the game. Starting well is helpful, but it's not always how you start the game, it's how you finish.

The best basketball games are those when one team comes from behind to win the game. It's not how you start, it's how you finish. You owe it to yourself to run hard and finish strong. You may or may not score. That depends on your skill set, what you've practiced, and the will of God; however, you would be positioned for success, with your odds of scoring increased. The basketball itself can be your life, your purpose, your relationship, your friendships, your marriage, your finances, or your welfare. Whatever it is, the best way to keep the enemy from stealing and destroying it with pressure is to give it to Jesus. Get involved with Christ. He's the center of all joy!

The enemy has had his hands on anything and everything that is purposeful to you. It's time for you to protect what's yours and that for which you were created. It's time to put the answers to those questions in practice. Make them a reality. Who are you? Where are you going? What's stopping you from getting there? The clock is ticking, and I don't know what quarter of your life you're in. … Neither do you because God ultimately makes the decision. So don't waste time. Imagine where you could be right now if you hadn't got stuck in the corner.

While there are lessons learned in the corner, there's also time ticking away. Your time is now. Generations are depending on you! Make the decision to break the press today. Step-thru it like the Children of Israel did. Reverse it or swing it like the Prodigal son did. Protect it like Sampson should've done. Run hard like Paul did! This is a war with many battles. It's an everlasting playoff between you and the enemy. You've been trapped in the corner long enough. It's time to press the release lever and loosen those strongholds on your life.

Remember, anything that you can hold, you can control. Remaining in the grips of the Enemy will lead to utter destruction. Swing the ball! Stay in-bounds! Fill the lane! Run hard because you should want to get to the fast-break. Your breakthrough is simply a pass away. Give it to Jesus, He's running point guard in my life. What about yours?

www.ingramcontent.com/pod-product-compliance
Lightning Source LLC
Chambersburg PA
CBHW071432040426
42445CB00012BA/1350